M000085561

Margaret Bourke-White
Photographer
by Judy Nayer

Scott Foresman

Editorial Offices: Glenview, Illinois • New York, New York
Sales Offices: Reading, Massachusetts • Duluth, Georgia
Glenview, Illinois • Carrollton, Texas • Menlo Park, California

Growing Up

Margaret Bourke-White was born in the Bronx, New York, on June 14, 1904. Her father, Joseph White, was an engineer and inventor who worked for a printing company. He worked very hard and was always striving for perfection. Her mother, Minnie Bourke, was an avid reader who valued books and learning.

When Margaret was four years old, her family moved to Bound Brook, New Jersey, to be closer to the factory where her father worked. They lived in a big house surrounded by trees and fields, with woods and streams nearby. Margaret Bourke-White's parents both loved nature. They wanted Margaret, her older sister, and her younger brother to love plants and wildlife as much as they did.

But Margaret was a fearful child. The first time her father put a caterpillar into her hands, she screamed and flung it away.

Margaret's parents had strong ideas about such things. They believed that learning to do things without fear was important.

"Face your fears," her mother would say, "and then do something."

To cure Margaret of her fears, her father took her on long nature walks, teaching her everything he knew about birds, bugs, reptiles, and other living things. Before long, Margaret's curiosity was sparked. She became excited by all that she saw in nature, and began exploring on her own. She collected insects and caterpillars, frogs and toads, and even snakes. Her father had to teach her which kinds were harmless, and which were dangerous.

One summer, Margaret raised two hundred caterpillars in her house. She waited to see them become moths or butterflies. Margaret had many pets, including hamsters, turtles, and rabbits, but her favorite pets were two snakes—a boa constrictor and a puff adder. By the time she was ten years old, she dreamed she would become a herpetologist— an expert on snakes and reptiles. She wrote in her diary that she pictured herself traveling to the jungles of foreign lands in search of rare snakes, "doing all the things that women never do."

Margaret first learned about photography from her father. He loved taking photographs. He took thousands of pictures of the family, his inventions, and the wildlife around their house. He experimented with different lenses and with the printing process. Although Margaret never used a camera herself when she was growing up, she spent many hours alongside her father as he took pictures. She even helped him develop his prints.

Margaret also went with her father on trips to the factories where he helped set up printing presses. Mr. White loved machines. He told her that machines were as beautiful as nature. When Margaret was eight years old, her father took her to the foundry where the presses were made. At a foundry, iron and other materials are melted to make steel. The steel is then molded into machine parts.

At first, it was so dark inside that Margaret couldn't see anything. But then, she said, "in a rush the blackness was broken by a sudden magic of flowing metal and flying sparks. I can hardly describe my joy. To me at that age, a foundry represented the beginning and end of all beauty." Margaret never forgot this scene. Later, when Margaret Bourke-White became a photographer, her first and favorite subjects were factories and machines.

Both of Margaret's parents had high standards and expectations. They expected their children to have important ambitions, and to be the best at whatever they did. Her father taught her to be determined. When Margaret had difficulty doing something, he would tell her to keep trying. "You can," he would say. Her mother taught her to be curious and fearless. "Open all the doors," she would say. Margaret would grow up to follow her parents' advice. She would do many things that at first seemed too difficult and open many doors that at first were closed.

Making Choices

After high school, Bourke-White went to Columbia University in New York. She was only seventeen. She was enjoying her first year in college when her father suddenly died. It was a terrible shock. Soon after, Bourke-White found herself turning to photography—perhaps because it had been her father's favorite hobby.

In addition to her science classes, Bourke-White took a class with Clarence H. White, one of the finest photographers of the time. Bourke-White's father had left the family with very little money. Still, when her mother heard of Bourke-White's interest in photography, she managed to buy a camera.

At that time, people were still deciding whether photography was an art, or just a matter of learning to use a new piece of equipment. Clarence White felt photography was an art. He taught his students to make photographs that looked almost like paintings. Bourke-White began to develop an artist's eye.

That summer, Bourke-White got a job as the photography and nature counselor at a camp in Connecticut. To make extra money, she also started her first photography business. She took pictures of the camp and the campers, and made picture postcards out of them. She sold them to parents and tourists. She did not estimate that she would sell so many, but by the end of the summer, she had printed almost two thousand pictures!

Bourke-White's main interest was still science. In 1922 she went to the University of Michigan to study herpetology. There she met Everett Chapman, another student who shared her interests. In 1924, Bourke-White left school and married Chapman.

But the marriage only lasted two years. Bourke-White returned to school, this time at Cornell University in New York. Although Bourke-White was still signed up for science classes, she starting taking photographs of the university's buildings to help pay for expenses. Bourke-White spent most of her time roaming the campus, taking photographs from every angle. She sold the pictures to students and teachers. Soon she found herself much more interested in photography than snakes. She decided that photography would be her life's work.

After college, Bourke-White moved to Cleveland, Ohio, a booming industrial city. She hoped to get a job as an architectural photographer there and take pictures of buildings. Bourke-White set up a studio in her one-room apartment. She used the kitchen as her darkroom, and washed her prints in the bathtub.

It didn't take long for Bourke-White to get work. She took pictures of banks, gardens, homes, and other buildings. Some of her pictures were published in magazines.

Bourke-White's favorite place in Cleveland was the Flats. It was an area of steel mills, factories, and railroad yards. Most people thought this area was ugly. But Bourke-White remembered the factory trips she had taken with her father. Once again, she saw beauty in industry.

Bourke-White loved the huge smokestacks that rose up from the furnaces in the steel mills, and took many photographs of them. She wanted to go inside the steel mills, but women were not allowed to do this. As she would do time and time again throughout her life, Bourke-White persisted. At last, she got permission to photograph the mill with the help of a friend, who wrote a letter to the president of Otis Steel. Bourke-White's prediction was accurate; her life would involve "doing all the things that women never do."

Bourke-White may have thought the hard part was over, but the real work was just beginning. Carrying her large, heavy camera equipment, she balanced high on narrow ledges and got dangerously close to the fiery, molten steel. But none of the pictures came out. The lighting was too poor inside the mill. Night after night, she and her friend Alfred Bemis searched for the exact spot and for the light that would give her a picture. They tried to estimate how much light she needed. Bourke-White tried every lens and every angle she could think of, but it seemed as though the problems were too great to solve. Just when time was running out, Bourke-White got a lucky break. Alfred met someone with new equipment—huge flares that were to be used to make movies. The flares worked. Bourke-White's pictures showed the flame and sparks of the liquid metal as it was poured.

The president of Otis Steel loved the pictures. No one had ever photographed the making of steel before. He put the photographs in a book called *The Story of Steel*, and Bourke-White gained recognition almost overnight.

Fame and Fortune

In 1929, Henry Luce, publisher of *Time* magazine, saw Bourke-White's steel photographs and was very impressed. He was starting a new magazine for business and industry that would feature photographs. For the first time, pictures would be as important as words. He offered Bourke-White a job taking the big, dramatic photographs needed for such a magazine, which would be called *Fortune*. Bourke-White felt as if the job had been created for her. After accepting it, she wrote to her mother, "I feel as if the world has been opened up and I hold all the keys."

Indeed, Bourke-White was to open up many doors as she worked for *Fortune*. The first story sent her to the stockyards of Chicago, where she took the photographs for a story on the meat-packing industry. "Hogs" became the lead story in the first issue of the magazine. Later it got recognition as one of the very first photo essays.

Bourke-White also photographed New York City's Chrysler Building as it was being built. To take the pictures, she stood with her camera and tripod on an open scaffold, eight hundred feet up in the air, as cold winds blew. Then, when the Chrysler Building was finished, she rented a studio behind the gargoyles that decorated the sixty-first floor of the building. She liked to climb out on the gargoyles and take pictures of the city. Soon Bourke-White became famous not only for her pictures, but for her daring exploits. Throughout her life, she would take great risks to get the pictures she wanted.

By 1930, many photographers started using the new, small, hand-held cameras that had come out. But Bourke-White stuck with her large, heavy cameras and bulky equipment. She felt they gave her more detailed, accurate pictures that defined her style.

Bourke-White spent half the year working for *Fortune*, and the other half on advertising jobs. She photographed ice cream, cars, tires, nail polish, and airplanes. Although she preferred her assignments with *Fortune*, these jobs earned her a small fortune!

Bourke-White opened yet another door when she photographed factories being built in Russia. No foreign photographer had ever been allowed to take pictures there. At first the answer was no, but that only made Bourke-White more determined. She said, "Nothing attracts me like a closed door. I cannot let my camera rest until I have pried it open." Bourke-White was finally allowed to take pictures wherever she wished. In fact, she made several trips to Russia, and the people there loved her. At age twenty-nine, she was on her way to becoming one of the most famous photographers in the world.

Life's Lessons

In 1934, Bourke-White was assigned by *Fortune* to take pictures of the Dust Bowl— the area in the midwest that was in a great drought. Millions of farm people were left homeless and penniless. For the first time, Bourke-White was moved by the people she was photographing. "I had never seen people caught helpless like this in total tragedy," she said. "These were faces I could not pass by." This was a turning point in her life. After returning from the Dust Bowl, she found it nearly impossible to go back to taking pictures of things like ice cream and cars when so many people were suffering. Soon, she decided to close her advertising studio. Now she would mainly photograph people.

The next year, Bourke-White traveled all over the South with a writer named Erskine Caldwell. They photographed and talked to the poor farmers there. Together they made a book called *You Have Seen Their Faces*, which showed how bad conditions in America were.

That same year, Henry Luce was starting yet another magazine—*Life*—which would tell the news through pictures. There would be very little writing, and even more photographs than *Fortune*. Bourke-White joined *Life* when it was formed in 1936, the only woman photographer on staff. For the next twenty-one years, she would travel far and wide for *Life*. Her photographs would help Americans see the world's most important events.

For its first issue, *Life* sent Bourke-White to photograph the Fort Peck Dam in Montana. The magazine was a huge success. It sold out at the newsstands within minutes. Bourke-White loved *Life* too. She would go anywhere and take any risk to get the pictures the magazine wanted.

On the Front Lines

Bourke-White would take her greatest risks in the upcoming years. In 1941, Europe was at war. *Life* predicted that Germany was about to invade Russia. Bourke-White was ready to be on the scene. It took weeks to get permission to photograph the war, but Bourke-White finally succeeded. She was the only photographer in Moscow when the Germans attacked. Bourke-White climbed on top of the American embassy. As bombs exploded all around her, she managed to take great pictures.

Months later, the United States entered World War II. In 1942 Bourke-White asked to be assigned to the war. She wore an officer's uniform and was given the rank of lieutenant. She was the first female military photographer in the war.

As she continued to photograph scenes of
the war, her legend grew. She survived when
her ship was torpedoed and sunk, and she
had to row away on a lifeboat. She was given
special permission to go on an actual bombing
mission in Africa. And she took pictures day
after day on the front lines in Italy, in the
middle of some of the most dangerous fighting
of the war. *Life*'s readers eagerly looked
forward to each new adventure.

The Last Assignments

In 1946, *Life* sent Bourke-White to India. They wanted her to cover India's struggle for independence from Great Britain. Bourke-White was to photograph India's leader, Mahatma Gandhi.

When Bourke-White arrived, she was told by Gandhi's secretary that she must first learn how to use a spinning wheel. The spinning wheel was symbolic of India's fight for freedom. Under British law, Indians were not allowed to make their own cloth; they had to buy it from Great Britain. Gandhi wanted Indians to spin their own thread and weave their own cloth so Great Britain would not profit from them.

Bourke-White was impatient, but she did learn to spin. She was told that she could use only three flashbulbs, and she could not speak to Gandhi because this was his day of silence. Despite these conditions, Bourke-White took a photograph of Gandhi that was so good it became world famous.

In 1949, Bourke-White was sent to South Africa, where she traveled two miles underground into a gold mine to photograph the black men who were forced to work there. The conditions in the mine were suffocating. Her pictures accurately depicted the plight of the exploited workers there.

Bourke-White's last war assignment was in 1952 in Korea, where the United States was involved in the war between North and South Korea. When she came home, she began to experience aches and pains, and she had trouble walking.

In 1954, she was diagnosed as having Parkinson's disease, an illness that affects the nervous system. For years she fought against her illness with the same determination that she displayed in all of her assignments.

Although she kept it a secret for a long time, eventually she told of her struggle with the disease, hoping that it would help other people.

By 1960, the age of the photo essay was ending. Television was taking over, and "The Margaret Bourke-White Story" aired as a television special that same year. Finally, after fighting Parkinson's disease for almost twenty years, Bourke-White died on August 27, 1971.

It is hard to believe that this adventurous photographer was the same fearful child who once screamed at the sight of a little, fuzzy caterpillar. During her life, Margaret Bourke-White fulfilled her dream of "doing all the things that women never do." Not only did she become one of the world's most famous photographers, but she also paved the way for many others. Bourke-White's legend lives on in her photographs, which record some of the most important events and people of the twentieth century.